101 NATURE JOKES

THE HENNESSY KIDS

THE HENNESSY ENTERTAINMENT COMPANY

101 Nature Jokes / by The Hennessy Kids

ISBN 978-1-989621-02-8 (Print)

ISBN 978-1-989621-03-5 (E-book)

1. Wit and humor, Juvenile. 2. English wit and humor. I. The Hennessy Kids, author

The Hennessy Entertainment Company | HennessyEnt.com |

Copyright © 2022 by The Hennessy Entertainment Company

All rights reserved.

No part of this book may be reproduced in any form or by any electronic or mechanical means, including information storage and retrieval systems, without written permission from the author, except for the use of brief quotations in a book review.

For Janet, a great caretaker of animals and nature.

1

BIRD JOKES

What bird can you buy at the grocery store?
A kiwi.

What brand of soap do birds use?
Dove.

What do you call a bunch of chickens playing hide-and-seek?
Fowl play.

What do you call a sick eagle?
Illegal.

What do you get if you cross a duck with fireworks?
A firequacker.

What do you give a sick bird?

Tweetment.

What does a bird like in his salad?

Crowtons.

What is a parrot's favourite game?

Hide and speak.

What kind of animal is a chickadee in winter?

A brrrrrd.

What kind of bird can carry the most?

The crane.

What kind of bird doesn't need a comb?

A bald eagle.

What kind of bird works at a construction site?

A crane.

What kind of bird works underground?

A mynah bird.

What kind of books do owls like?
Hoot-dunits.

What kind of math do owls like?
Owlgebra.

What's another name for a smart-alecky duck?
A wise quacker.

When do teachers carry crackers?
On parrot-teacher conference days.

When should you buy a bird?
When it's goes cheep.

Where do birds invest their money?
In the stork market.

Which bird is out of breath all the time?
A puffin.

Why did the bird want to join the army?
He wanted to be a parrot trooper.

Why did the pelican bring a lot of money to the restaurant?

Because he had a very big bill.

Why do crows sit on telephone poles?

To make long distance caws.

Why do I hear the song "You Need To Calm Down" coming from my fireplace?

You have a Taylor chimney swift.

Why does a flamingo lift up one leg?

Because if it lifted both legs it would fall over.

2

BUG JOKES

Why would you call the police get rid of bugs?
Because they have a S.W.A.T. team.

How do bees brush their hair?
With a honey comb.

How do bees get to school?
They take the buzz.

What do you say to start a firefly race?
Ready. Set. Glow.

How do fleas travel?
They itch-hike.

What did old caterpillars use to order Christmas gifts?
Cater-logs.

What did one girl firefly say to the other girl firefly?
You glow, girl.

What did the sushi roll say to the bee?
Wassabee.

What do ants use to smell better?
Deodor-ant.

What do bees say when they get back to their hive?
"Honey, I'm back."

What do fireflies eat?
Light snacks.

What do moths study in school?
Mothematics.

What do you call a bee's bum?
It's bee-hind.

What do you call a beetle that can dance?
A jitterbug.

What do you call a bug that can't have too much sugar?
A diabeetle

What do you call a bug that jumps inside your cupboard?
A glasshopper.

What do you call a cricket that takes pictures?
A shutterbug.

What do you call a funny chicken?
A comedi-hen

What do you call a really old ant?
An antique.

What do you call a wasp?
A wanna-bee.

What do you call two spiders who just got married?
Newlywebs.

What do you do with a sick wasp?
Take it to the waspital.

What do you get when you cross an insect and a rabbit?
Bugs Bunny.

What insect are you most likely to find in school?
A spelling bee.

What is a bug's favourite sport?
Cricket.

What is a caterpillar scared of?
A dog-erpillar.

What is a mosquito's favourite sport?
Skin diving.

What is worse than finding half a worm in your apple?
Spitting the other half out.

What kind of bugs live in clocks?
Ticks.

What kind of car do bugs like to drive?
A Volkswagen Beetle.

What was the best bug band ever?
The Beatles.

What was the spider doing on the computer?
Searching the web.

What's a caterpillar's favourite weapon?
A cater-polt.

When do spiders go on their honeymoon?
After their webbing day.

Where do ants go for winter vacation?
Antarctica.

Where's the best place to buy bugs?
A flea market.

Why are spiders good at computer safety?
They catch bugs on the web.

THE HENNESSY KIDS

Why did the boy throw butter out the window?
To see butter fly.

Why did the fly fly?
Because the spider spied her.

Why didn't the butterfly want to go to the dance?
Because she heard it was a moth ball.

Why do humming birds hum?
Because they can't remember the words.

Why don't people like bed bugs?
Because they get under their skin.

Why is the centipede always late for school?
Well, just think of all the shoes it has to put on.

Why was the fly looking for the garbage can?
Because he was a litterbug.

Why was the grocery store out of butter?
Because butter flies.

3

PLANT & TREE JOKES

Did you know I can cut a tree down just by looking at it?
It's true. I saw it with my own eyes.

Do you want a brief explanation of an acorn?
In a nutshell, it's an oak tree.

How did the dummy get hurt while raking leaves?
He fell out of the tree.

How do trees access the internet?
They log on.

How do trees resolve arguments?
They sign a tree-ty.

How do you identify a dogwood tree?
By its bark.

How was the acorn feeling after it was buried?
It was feeling oak-ay.

I asked my dad,"Would you ever go on all-cashew diet?"
He said,"No, that's just nuts."

What did the Jedi knight say to the sacred tree?
May the forest be with you.

What did the tree do when the bank closed?
It started its own branch.

What did the trees wear to the pool party?
Swimming trunks.

What do you get when you cross a cat with a lemon tree?
A sour puss.

What do you give to a sick citrus tree?
Lemon aid.

What gets a year older whenever it rings?
A tree.

What happens to the romantic trees every Valentine's Day?
They get sappy.

What is a tree's favourite part of math?
Treegonometree.

What is a tree's least favourite month?
Sep-timberrrr.

What is a tree's favourite shape?
A treeangle.

What is the same shape as a tall pine tree but weighs nothing?
The shadow of a tall pine tree.

What kind of a tree do science teachers plant?
Chemist-tree.

What kind of flowers will grow when you plant kisses?
Tulips.

What kind of tree grows chickens?

Poultree.

What kind of tree fits right in your hand?

A palm tree.

What weighs more: a pound of leaves or a pound of logs?

They both weigh exactly the same amount.

Did you hear the famous noisy bird walking through the leaves?

It was Rustle Crow.

When are trees less stressed out?

In spring, when they are releaved.

Where do young trees go to learn?

Elementree school.

Which tree radio station plays all today's musical hits?

Poplar FM.

Which trees miss the most school days because of colds and flu?

The sycamore.

Why do you say leaves are risk-takers?
They are always out on a limb, that's why.

Which tree has the most friends?
The poplar one.

Why did a bunch of trees all take a nap at the same time?
For rest.

Why was the pine tree in a bad mood at Christmas?
Because it was on Santa's knotty list.

Why do dogwood trees make good pets?
They have a nice bark, but they wooden bite.

Why do trees hate lumberjack tests?
Because they get stumped.

Why do trees make the worst enemies?
Because they are really good at throwing shade.

Which city do trees go to when they want to watch a hockey game?
Montreeal.

GO ADVENTURE

ENJOY THE OUTDOORS

RESPECT NATURE

READY TO DO NATURALLY FUN ACTIVITIES?

HERE YOU GO: A WORD SEARCH, AN OWL TO COLOUR, A FLOWER MANDALA TO COLOUR, PLUS HELP A BUTTERFLY GET THROUGH A MAZE BACK TO ITS HOME!

```
D  S  Y  H  C  R  I  B  D  M
B  P  L  N  P  O  P  L  A  R
G  I  F  D  N  S  B  E  N  O
U  D  R  O  A  U  L  E  D  W
B  E  E  W  X  G  B  D  E  L
Y  R  T  Y  A  J  E  U  L  B
D  F  T  E  A  N  T  C  I  E
A  I  U  K  W  A  H  K  O  N
L  R  B  B  E  A  R  Y  N  I
C  H  I  C  K  A  D  E  E  P
```

Ant	Chickadee	Ladybug
Bear	Dandelion	Owl
Bee	Duck	Pine
Birch	Eagle	Poplar
Blue jay	Fir	Spider
Bunny	Fox	Wasp
Butterfly	Hawk	Worm

4

ABOUT DALY POINT NATURE RESERVE

If you are ever travelling by Bathurst, New Brunswick, you are invited to stop by Daly Point Nature Reserve. It is one of the only places in the world where the Maritime Ringlet butterfly can be found.

And be sure to bring bird seed or shelled unsalted peanuts if you take the trail to chickadee landing, because the black-capped chickadees will land right on your hand to grab those snacks.

5

YOUR FAVOURITE JOKE

What is your favourite nature joke that isn't in this book?

Send it to us at thehennessykids@gmail.com, and we'll look to share it online with all our friends!

Thank you for reading our book! We hope you enjoyed it. Please tell these jokes to your friends and family and make more people happy.

ABOUT THE AUTHOR

The Hennessy Kids think the world would be better with more smiles.

Want to know when our new books are available? Sign up for our **Fun Stuff With Heart** newsletter at HennessyEnt.com!

BOOKS BY THE HENNESSY KIDS

101 Halloween Jokes

101 Christmas Jokes

101 Pet Jokes

101 Knock Knock Jokes, Vol. 1

101 Nature Jokes

101 Food Jokes

www.ingramcontent.com/pod-product-compliance
Lightning Source LLC
Chambersburg PA
CBHW071255070526
44583CB00017B/2483